American Prophet

Edited by Peter Markus
Book design by Daniel Marlow
Cover photograph by MaryClare Peak

Marick Press
P.O. Box 36253
Grosse Pointe Farms, Michigan 48236
www.marickpress.com

Printed and bound in Canada

Library of Congress Cataloging-in-Publication Data
Fanning, Robert
American Prophet
Poems in English
ISBN 978-1-934851-01-2

MARICK
PRESS

American Prophet

poems

Robert Fanning

*—for Denise and Gabriel
and Magdalena*

Contents

The Sea of Faith
Was once, too, at the full, and round Earth's shore
Lay like the folds of a bright girdle furled.
But now I only hear
Its melancholy, long, withdrawing roar,
Retreating, to the breath
Of the night-wind, down the vast edges drear
And naked shingles of the world.

—Matthew Arnold

A world war
Was announced
Days ago
But they didn't know...

Religions fall.
Children shelled.
(Children shelled?)
That's all very well,

But would you please
keep the noise down low
because you're waking
the lazy sunbathers...

—Morrissey

THE PROPHET AT THE DRY CLEANERS

Announcing his entrance, the dull rattle of bells
over the door. An old woman emerges
from the back, from another world
of hissing machinery and steam. Handing her
a pink slip, the Prophet does not ask:
Isn't our flesh a garment heavy enough...?
nor try to smooth her wrinkled face. In a blink
she's gone, and soon the metal rack lurches,
snaking down toward him, dragging its cargo
of starched shirts, trousers, floral blouses, dresses.
Tagged and wrapped in plastic bags,
hundreds of faceless men, women and children
descend in their wedding gowns
and business suits, their Sunday best.
No more shit, soil, or blood in their fabric.
Inaudible beneath the screech of bearings
and pulleys, the intermittent dragon roar
of the steam press, he says: *There will be peace
when this fashion show is over...*when the machine stops
and the woman draws his black suit from the rack.
There are pulls in the breast, she says,
lifting the bag to show beneath the lapel
where his black threads unravel, a hole
worn clean through. Then, in her own torn voice
she tells him the price he will pay.

1

THE PROPHET'S LAMENT AT SPRING BREAK

Standing on the diving board in his black shoes
and suit, the Prophet casts his hand's shadow
on the curved globe of the huge party beach ball
but no one heeds. *Enough of this blind reverie...*
he shouts, but can't outdo the pink radio on full blast,
the diva's citrus wail. Hoisting a bruised apple,
he offers: *The gnawed heart of this nation...*
but fades, momentarily lost in the oil-slicked curves
and belly rings, all the licking and jiggling,
the tattooed machismo, the orgiastic thump
of thundering bass, tangled teen lovers rolling
like carp in the shallow end, the cannonball splash,
the squirt gun war. As he booms: *This false palace teeters
on a rotten foundation...*the Prophet fights the fleeting
thought that life *is* short, that maybe they're *right*
to splash and giggle, right to be blind
to the clouds of ash billowing from their burning
cities, soon to swallow the sun, right to ignore
the lifeguard, the glaring signs. Poolside, a dropped
Bomb Pop sits stick up in the stain of its spilled flag.
And on the pool's surface, the dance of flickering,
marbled light, the glazed citizens bobbing
on inflatable dinosaurs, out beyond rescue.

THE PROPHET AT ELVISFEST

Beneath the certain stars, this field
in Ypsilanti is filled with aged,
greased believers, dolled-up grandmas,
gleaming muscle cars. Descending the hill
in his black suit, the Prophet, too, has come

to see the King. Raised in another time,
he stands outside the glow that lights the faces
of the gathered throng, curious and a world apart.
On wet grass, the die-hard worshippers all rise
from folding chairs, all eyes on the mobile

rent-a-stage as the first Elvis, inevitably
in diapers the day the real King died,
mounts the stage. Soon enough, *Hound Dog* howls
through the crackling amps as this King,
coiffed and sneering, twists his leather hips

on well-oiled bearings. All the old gals wail.
And so begins this litany of hits,
a barrage of oldies hours into the night,
as each of seven Elvises revisits
a different era of the King. In a brief lull

prior to the arrival of the last King, the Prophet
ascends the stage, not to sing, but to deliver them
a simple message. Pointing toward the sky,
he begins: *Believers, see how the blue moon wanes...*
but when he sees they're unmoved, he taps

the mic, confused. He wavers, but continues,
louder: *How will we know the voice
of a true King among us?* Distracted, they stare
elsewhere, and for a moment
the Prophet knows how Elvis

must have felt near the end, numbed,
staring out through the haze at a sea
of strangers, his voice rising faint
and unrecognizable in the distant radio
station of his chest. Just then, parting waves

of fans in a huge, high-finned cruiser,
the evening's King of Kings arrives,
a glittering whale in tight white polyester.
His bell bottoms shush as he passes
through hushed watchers, savior

in a pompadour and dark glasses, belly
rippling with rhinestones, heavyweight belt
of false gold, handful of faux silk scarves.
Holding a wireless mic, he croons *I Can't Help
Falling in Love with You*, stopping at a woman

lost in the middle of the crowd who watches from
a wheelchair. Bending toward her like some carnival
preacher or evangelist, he wraps the scarf around
her neck as she closes her eyes, still afflicted,
offering her face to the small miracle of his kiss.

THE PROPHET IN THREATENING WEATHER

As he sleeps, something tugs the bell rope
in his tower of a dream, so, alarmed, the Prophet
rises and turns to the sea. Awakened, he walks
a hulking dune to the cliff, takes for his crow's nest

a vacant lighthouse from where he watches.
Already the moon is down deep in the ocean's throat.
Toward the sleeping shore town he feels
a morning storm loom. Somewhere a front

of ripped thunderheads, heaped miles out,
leans its blue-grey shoulders toward the beach.
Standing in his black suit in this lonely helm
at the edge of the Earth, the Prophet lifts

a telescope and through splintered glass windows
sees it coming: mounting waves and distant ropes
of rain. Yet it's all hovering, and soon a bright
morning still arrives without warning—a swift rise

and, clockwork, the sun rings in its loft of sky
calling all worshippers to another day of bathing,
paperbacks and castles. Up the beach, he sees
the staff of bronzed lifeguards mount their thrones

with whistles and lotion. For a moment,
sweat beading beneath his black suit, lifting his arms
to shout as he watches children dive and disappear
in chopped currents, the Prophet remembers

the scene soon into *Jaws 2*: Roy Scheider, shocked,
eyeing shallow and offshore a sinister shape
of what he would learn later was just a shifting
school of fish, and yelling *SHARK! SHARK!*

Result: seismic waves of panic, a chorus
of blood-curdling screams. So, though sure
of the sharp weather cutting toward his people,
the Prophet lowers his dark arms and holds his breath.

THE PROPHET AT THE MATINEE

In the final hour, just before the meteor shower
to end all meteor showers—as the wannabe hero
stands in his zippered flight jacket on the deck,
pledging with his crew to accomplish

the mission of saving Earth or at least America:
cut to wide-angle shot of an intergalactic
boulder bigger than Texas, one of a million
hurtling space turds determined to reduce

the world to rubble, while down in the dark
theater, the watchers hunker in stadium seats,
surround sound shaking the walls and floor,
suddenly unsure their crew of handsome astronauts

and lasers will do the trick. In the end it's precision
missiles versus rocks and it's clear the rocks will win:
shot of a sonic shock-wave, D.C. doused in flame,
the President and his cabinet watching this

apocalyptic brushfire rush across the continent
through the portholes of satellite TV monitors, safe
in their subterranean bunker. And they who've dropped
fifteen bucks on a ticket and popcorn combo

watch too, through the cinema's wall-sized screen
New York and L.A. blown to smithereens, as some
invisible God hurls a skyful of giant pebbles
on their glittering cities. But of course it's all

a dream; before final credits roll, the hero hits snooze
on his clock radio after hearing the President's address:
some shift in universal winds averted the storm's course
into deep space. The last shot shows champagne corks

popping all around the world—a ticker tape blizzard
in slo-mo, lovers embracing, Earthlings lifting
their glasses to incredible fate. And after
it's over, the Prophet stands outside the theater

in his black suit watching the faces of his people
break into the stark fact of daylight and the parking lot,
their eyes adjusting to the glare, glad to see for now
the wide sky clear and the world still here.

THE PROPHET AT THE SUPERSTORE

In this fluorescent cathedral, the Prophet's lost
in the walled maze of aisles between Small Appliances
and Housewares, trying to find a night-light
for his bedroom, when he hears air raid sirens
and screams somewhere in the direction
of the Boy's and Men's Department.
In his black suit, he walks briskly toward

Boy's and Men's but sees no sign of bombing.
No seeming skirmish in Petites and Misses,
no battle near Lingerie, Jewelry, Footwear,
or the Cafeteria, but somewhere, again, a missile
whistles overhead, another explosion,
and he knows deep in his heart there's a war.
Passing Lawn and Garden, he hears more

hissing tracers, catches scattered blooms
of green anti-aircraft fire lighting up the sky
in the gold framed mirrors of Home and Office.
Turning into Electronics, he sees his people
leaning on their carts, some in awe, others gleeful
and beaming, all gawking at a flickering wall:
dozens of televisions all tuned to the same

laser-guided fireworks display.
The kid behind the counter, universal remote
in hand, cranks the volume, showing off
the surround sound. On his chest, a button
reads *Service Guaranteed*. Nearby, a grandma
holds two kids close; short, they all watch the war
on the half-off, cable-ready, 13" black and white

with built-in VCR. Most hover near the middle row
eyeing the 50" diagonal, wide-screen, HDTV
plasma monitor, where now a simmering crowd
all chants in sync, parading the torched Stars
and Stripes. The network then cuts to a shot
of the President at his desk in the Oval Office;
many-faced, his mugs fill this wall of televisions—

looming, rouged and ruddy.
Hitting the power off on one TV, the Prophet turns
to the watchers, shouting: *My people, the time
is upon us! Here we stand face to face
with the mirrored eye of the fly
who leads us blindly into the Valley of Death…*
when a louder voice resounds from the high

ceiling speakers: *"Good evening, shoppers. Our store
will be closing in 5 minutes. Please take your final
selections to the registers."* Then the aisles begin
to darken and one by one the new TV screens,
clicked off, gone black as pools of oil, reflect
the diminishing bodies of the shoppers
as they sink, pulled by heavy carts.

THE PROPHET AT THE CASINO

One of many pilgrims arriving at the shore's
gilded empire of cash temples and pastel hotels,
the Prophet walks in his black suit across the Atlantic
City boardwalk toward the revolving doors,
spilling in with the seasonal spawn of small-time
tourists, the shiny coins of their faces rolling
across fish-eyed mirrors housing hidden
surveillance cameras that catch them

on film. Down long gleaming halls of this
strange heaven, smiles of washed-up teen angels
and has-been crooners glare from promo posters
as they pass. At the end of this corridor
an unworldly light emanates, as each hallway
in this circular hotel leads like a spoke into a core
where light from the gaming floor shoots upward
like a huge pneumatic tube, taking their deposits

straight to God. Reaching the shaft of this glass
and golden phallus, he stares through palm fronds
to the oculus like a rifle barrel's end aimed
into the mouth of deep space. As Luke Skywalker
must have, upon his arrival, the Prophet whispers
*So this is the Death Star...*awed by its gaudy
brilliance, a good moth drawn into its radiant web.
And oh, Darth, spider, how sticky intricate

and sweet death tastes here at the slot machine.
Lemon, lemon, lemon: a few pulls of the handle
and already the fruits of his labor align
in digital windows, stacked neatly as they are

in farm markets, tokens cheering into the silver tray,
a siren wail proclaiming him a winner,
one of the chosen. His blood a good
and rising American river, the Prophet

floats with Lady Luck to a table, eager
to raise the stakes. Fifty dollars later,
he's penniless again, a nobody in his thrift
store suit—staring down the row at the glowing
faces of his people, half-deaf to the bells
and jangling mayhem, their bodies dangling
like hunched cocoons from the machines, now
connected to the slots by thin umbilical

debit wires that feed from them as they drain
their savings on the hope of being saved.
Too spent tonight to play Christ in the temple
or Nicholas Cage in *Leaving Las Vegas*, to knock
the tables and takers over, broke and drunk
with righteousness, instead the Prophet
cuts his losses and turns—flushed straight down
the innards toward the exit. Leaving,

he walks to his car across the rooftop structure
where a high barbed wire fence keeps the monthly
suicide count down, admiring the stars' glint
of spare change scattered across the granite
fountain floor of the night sky, and makes
one wish, not for what he's lost to return,
but for what he might save, and with this,
turns in his suit and walks away.

THE PROPHET AT THE LIFESAVING COURSE

Answering the call of an ad on the wall
at the grocery store, the Prophet enlists
for a lifesaving lesson at the local pool.
Entering the shallow end with the rest

of the students, he stands waist high
in his black swimsuit, clutching the ladder.
In an emergency, you cannot buy
any time, the instructor says, *consider*

the tides, how waves move, save your breath.
In a three-hour course he covers glide and crawl,
lake and ocean rescues, pool traumas, methods
of lifting, resuscitation. *Never take this calling*

lightly, he barks, *the minute you look away, danger*
happens. His chance to try a save, the Prophet grasps
for the falling dummy in the deep end, injures
his groin as he flails to reach it. Choked, gasping,

carried to the side by the guard, he eyes through
flooded goggles the caged wall clock, its arms
waving in distress. *No time for failed rescues,*
coughs the Prophet, *no time for false alarms.*

THE PROPHET AND THE SURGERY OF LIGHT

Scanning his online horoscope one night,
the Prophet's amazed at his potential:
a favorable year of great investments,
the prospect of long-term love all but assured
as long as he doesn't make any rash decisions
and keeps a bright outlook. Scrolling down
with a smile—a sizzle then a loud pop,
as his terminal buzzes, the microwave flashes
midnight, and sparks rain down from a blown
transformer nearby. Standing, he walks across
the sudden dark of his room to the window,
sees one blackened square—one unlit block
in an otherwise bright city. Donning his
black suit, he leaves his building, walks
the streets until he comes upon a congregation
of trucks, where men in white coats come
and go, training flashlights on a utility pole
strung with wires, a crane ascending
toward the box knocked dead. Floodlit,
the pole's an electric crucifix high in the trees,
a spine these night surgeons climb to remove
a burnt vertebra, lowering it to the ground
for inspection. *What hope will revive this
paralysis of light*, thinks the Prophet,
watching for hours the busy electricians
welding and fusing. An hour before sunrise
they're up there again, hammering nails in deep,
reconnecting a new transformer to some far source,
as, *hallelujah*, the lights blink on. Heading home,
the Prophet lifts a threadbare leaf, its capillaries backlit
by a streetlight, asking: *Who's to say what's dead?*

THE PROPHET AND THE SYMPHONY OF BROKEN HORNS

Who conducts this dream in which
the Prophet leads with lifted baton
a tone-deaf marching band toward town?
Playing their *Symphony of Broken Horns*

they turn down Main and the crowd
of Sunday shoppers plugs their ears.
His drummer's off-time crescendo tumbles
to a chorus of warped woodwinds, tuba honk,

moan of old trombones. Miles from here,
down in a dark sea, blue whales turn
toward this song they know by heart
and swoon. These townspeople,

however, tuned into lite ballads
and one hit wonders, blindly bop
to radio pop, ignore the undertow
and shop, shop, shop. It's no surprise

they shiver at the symphony's arrival,
hurling curses at the bruised, heartfelt music.
In his black suit, the Prophet madly waves
his arms like Beethoven as they pass

The Gap, glad their din outdoes
the outdoor speakers someone's hung
in trees to hide the wind with a happy
soundtrack. Though ragged as a band

of smoke-draped fogies in a Civil War
re-enactment, they keep a brisk
Pied Piper pace: the town's hired snipers
hide in the chain bookstore attic,

try to pick them off one by one
as they turn the corner in their cavalcade.
But the sharpshooters' magic bullets
keep missing, and soon the symphony's

dissonant assault empties stores,
as the shoppers, grown too ruminant
to use their credit cards, drop
their wares and head toward home.

2

THE PROPHET IN FLIGHT

Tonight on an eastward red-eye flight across
the country, the Prophet witnesses through his porthole:
first the sundown's crimson dousing desert mesas,
then the dark sea pooling in canyons, night's flood

spilling into heartland farms where streetlights
shimmer few and far between. Through shredded sails
of cirrus a blood red moon rises on the horizon,
as, coming into view one bright city after another—

Chicago, Milwaukee, Cleveland, Detroit—their spilled
electric treasures glinting, shine upward as the plane
rides jet stream currents down. Delighted as a diver
discovering scattered gems, the Prophet stares,

amazed by tentacles of freeway light stretching for miles,
giant pulsing nets spread to defy the gulfs of darkness
between them and sees this vision: that with this
towering energy his people have erected great

blockades of light, that working together they've
transformed the tides to keep the night forever
at bay. Buoyant and elated, the Prophet knows
he must address his people. Standing, he smoothes

his black suit, moves into the aisle, and speaks:
My fellow passengers, beneath our silver wings now,
see how a great force carries forth in all directions...
Looking past him at the flickering movie screen,

rows of half-lit faces remain immersed in the in-flight
comedy, headsets on. Others doze open-mouthed,
some don't lift their eyes from crosswords or copies
of the complimentary *Sky Shopper* magazine. To capture

their attention, the Prophet turns his voice up a notch:
Those of you on the south side of the plane will now see
Detroit shining and see in its rising light a sign...
when something in him sinks, losing sight

of that city's lights outside the plane. Tossed with
sudden inner turbulence, he leans to look out
the emergency exit window toward the apparently
missing city, wobbling as the seatbelt sign flashes on

and the pilot soothes them, his voice humming like a father's
while blessing his infant good night: *we're now beginning*
our descent. Following orders, the Prophet takes
his seat, and places the metal clasp securely in its buckle.

THE PROPHET IN THE BLACKOUT

Sparked by visions of sun-flooded canyons
on last night's cross-country flight, tonight
the Prophet logs on, setting forth for the digital
frontier of the Internet, to see what he can discover.

Googling sites on Native American tribes
he finds the words of the Cherokee: "*To the North
the Great Spirit gave the white race
the Guardianship of the Fire...*"

As he clicks red links reading "*The Four Directions,*"
"*The Shaking of the Earth,*" "*The Gourd of Ashes,*"
a quick flutter of the lamps and his screen
and house go black. A shock of silence

stuns the world outside his locked room
and windows before his neighbors begin to fight
their panic, checking fuses, flicking switches,
seeking answers. *Oh my people*, he whispers,

gathering candles—looking for his black suit
in the closet, as voices through transistor static
speak of a sudden flare and system failure
at Niagara's Mohawk Plant. In a span of nine

minutes, New York, Toronto, Cleveland,
and Detroit are extinguished, as station to station,
the Northeast power grid's knocked out cold.
Early reports dismiss terrorism, witnesses

confirm a lightning strike, an hour later
every theory dims and the cause goes unknown.
But the Prophet knows early on, before
the superstore shelves empty of water and ice,

before the gas stations go dry and close, before
the sway of blackened streetlights, the wail
of sirens, that whether an act of God or man,
this is a blazing sign. Beneath the moon, he walks

toward the hush of streets under curfew, listens
to the blackout coverage on his handheld radio.
Silhouettes of busy workers haunt the shut
Shop-n-Save, as errant flashlight beams flick

fogged glass of freezer doors, peer into
register drawers, glance the huddled shapes
of trash bags filled with perishables. In the lot, a lone
gull stands on the shopping cart corral, looking west,

where beyond the houses and stores, broadcast towers,
normally thin fingers flashing their red jewels,
stick the sky like six black needles, tapped to drain
the moon. Leaving the streets, he sees in a distant field

a grounded star, and follows this halo of only light
to its source. Reaching the corona of an impromptu
campfire, the Prophet finds his people laughing, shouting
slurred across the flames. Like a cavalry of lost soldiers

far from the battlefield or cowboys in a spoof
Western, they drink and sing, joking about The End
of the World, lifting cans of beer, cups half full
of warm boxed wine. Outside their revelry

he stands and watches those closely, who between
sputtering laughs, taking swigs, can't stop the current
of fear, leaping now from face to face in a circuit
of uncertainty. Stepping closer to the circle,

the Prophet longs to tell them: *Guardians, now*
your lights are down, and with drink you douse
*the fire you'll need to guide you home…*but another
drinking game drowns the moment, so he turns toward

his own dark home. Late the next day, town by town,
thrown switches fill the lines again, and like a sedative
coursing through a network of veins, the electric buzz
begins to blur the blackout into memory.

Returning to the embers of last night's deserted camp,
the Prophet finds the revelers' whittled branch stabbing
scorched earth: an accidental sundial, shadow of a sharp
angled time, near miss of a flaming arrow aimed at their hearts.

THE PROPHET AND THE SUMMER FAIR

Where he finds his people gathered, the Prophet
will speak of the last great wind and the trust
of birds, he thinks, as he teeters into the gusts
like a crow, his black suit coat blowing
behind him. Closing his eyes, he spreads

his arms and imagines gliding toward where,
from the woods beyond town, he hears
the raffle and laughs of some summer fair.
Walking a road that follows the curve
of rapids, he sees the first sign, nailed to a tree

above a group of white deflated balloons,
pointing: *This Way to the Community Fair.*
Unable to cross where the river's grown wide
before the falls, the Prophet watches the fair
from the other side: rows of children,

some stepping gently, others in a jaunty dash,
trying to balance eggs on plastic spoons,
beckoned by cheering adults with blue ribbons.
Clowns follow close behind the little ones
with cartons of eggs. One kid's, then another's

topples and splats. Some try to catch the falling
ovals, one kneels over crushed fragments,
hands down in the golden goop, and starts to cry.
Cupping his hands to his mouth, the Prophet shouts:
Children, it will be like this for you

in the breaking days, carrying the fragile world
of your birth through the distance and wind...
but drowned by the river, the roar around
the ribbon winner, the honk of the clown's horn,
the Prophet's voice doesn't reach them,

except for one child who stops crying
and stands in the field of shattered eggs
looking across the river in his direction.
The race ending, he turns to receive another egg,
walking slowly, guarding it with his life.

THE PROPHET AT THE FESTIVAL OF KITES

At the shore the sky's a shattered
rainbow of kites, a bird whirling dream.
Faces skyward, a crowd giggles
and coos beneath a giant mobile.
Standing on the sand in his black suit
and shoes, the Prophet's arms extend
as his huge black kite ascends, occluding
the sun. To the rest it seems less
than a passing shadow, though drifting
in the middle of this kaleidoscope dawn,
it might be a giant ink stain, or one of those
first seaborne storm clouds, the harbor's
harbingers of coming rain. Like those
coastline planes pulling ads of half-off
seafood dinners or local haunt happy hour
specials, the Prophet's strung his kite tail
with one long message to his people,
each plastic marquee letter clattering
in the strong wind. But soon the weight
of his sentence sinks the kite. Finally,
here he stands in the middle of all this
shrill elation, his people pointing
to the sky, and across the sand
his dark clauses drag.

THE PROPHET AT THE BARN
LOOKING FOR THE FACE OF GOD

Dozens of worshippers trekked miles to stand here
this summer dusk, as they do each night, beside
a windblown cornfield in a Midwestern farm,
purple thunderheads billowing. The Prophet, too,
has trudged miles in his black suit through calf-high
tornadoes of dust and skittering tumbleweed.
As the last of the light like a seed drops

into August earth, somewhere in the dark barn
the farmer throws a switch, flooding the face
with light. A collective gasp, then weeping
and murmuring—as a strata of enlightenment
emerges: those who see Christ's face, those who
think they kind of sort of see it, and those who don't.
Strangers, they're suddenly nudging together

in a gathering storm, looking up at the barn,
rain beginning to pelt them. The crowd moves
a little right, the crowd moves a little left,
depending on the vantage point of whomever
claims the best view. The Prophet leans
close to one of the seers near him who points for one
of the blind toward the rainspout—*see, right there,*

that's the side of Christ's face. If you follow that
down the grain chute—see that hole between
the planks?—that's the pupil of the eye...
them hay bales is the moustache and beard.
See? See? Just then, a shriek—as one woman,
the first to see Christ's face, hits her knees, wailing:
He's crying, he's crying, the Lord is crying!

And yes indeed, as the man near the Prophet points out
to his confused acolytes, confirming the tears:
*See that gutter there? It's gushin'. All of a sudden,
it's gushin'.* Still seeing nothing but wood, nails,
stalls and bales, the Prophet steps into the beams
of light to face his people. As he begins: *My people,
let us reflect upon this face we seek, our own...*

they shout and curse at the farmer, pointing at
this sudden shadow which now disturbs their view.
Frantic, the farmer dashes to adjust the lights,
as, thunderclap and downpour, they all stampede
into the barn. Except for those few who see,
who writhe and moan now in pools of mud,
baptized by rain, a herd of kneeling swine.

THE PROPHET IN TRAFFIC

Off the exit ramp toward home, the Prophet
finds himself trapped in gridlock at the light.
Where are my people headed, he wonders,
watching their sullen faces through windows
as they inch ahead. Must be a funeral

for someone famous, he thinks, pulling into
the slow procession behind thousands of brake lights
in the rain. In his rearview mirror, two lanes
of headlights stretch for miles. But seeing
no orange flags on their hoods, no sign

of a hearse out ahead, and noticing they're
directed toward the domed stadium, he knows
it's no funeral. It must be Sunday's pilgrimage
to the football game. But why so late? Surely
the game's over. Before long, unable to change

lanes, he's missed his street, so continues,
bumper to bumper in the herd. Finally, at the gates,
men holding bouquets of cash point them
to empty spaces. Rolling his window down,
the Prophet stammers *I'm lost…*and asks how to leave

but the man yells *move ahead*, so he parks beside
a busload of men in black suits. On the side of the bus
in block letters, it reads: *1310 AM, Tune in and Find
the Way.* As he gets out of his car, the men wave
at him, standing confused in his black suit, watching

thousands filing through turnstiles into the stadium.
In lights, above the bright gates where they enter,
a sign reads: *Welcome, Sons and Daughters of the Way.*
Having no ticket, he gets back in his car and stares
through his fogged window at the gathering

of believers huddled in hooded parkas in line.
Heads bowed, they pray and sing in unison, as one man
lifts his arms, conducting their voices. Above them
the domed arena looms, luminescent and ominous
as the alien mother ship in *Close Encounters*

of the Third Kind. Though wide-eyed and speechless,
the Prophet thinks *I'm no Richard Dreyfuss*, dreaming
of deliverance at the Devil's Tower while watching
his people fall prey to a celestial mass kidnapping,
hypnotized by stick figures. Nor will he sit here

and witness them disappear down the roaring gullet
of an arena to worship a false prophet who makes
six figures. Instead, the Prophet turns, making
his way back home, knowing this world's
the one where the work needs to be done.

THE PROPHET RETURNS HOME

At day's end, trudging up the sidewalk
to his apartment building, the Prophet sighs,
pulls keys from the pocket of his black suit coat.
The doorman looks through him as usual,
his eyes fixed on the door. On the elevator
the Prophet recollects his day, closing his eyes
to see the many beautiful faces of his people:
the man this morning holding his daughter
under an awning in a downpour, the woman
laughing while directing traffic. The bus stop
faces, the crosswalk faces, the drugstore faces,
the faces behind car windows, the faces
that seemed to see him, the faces looking down.
Opening his door, the Prophet enters
the stale familiar air, sees the tail of his black cat
sticking out from under the couch, the wrinkled light
falling through his window's web of plastic wrap
and duct tape, the La-Z-Boy, his stack
of Farmer's Almanacs, the TV with its crooked
rabbit ears. Dinner's predictable: a boxed
microwave meal, a glass of milk. Then the world
news, *Wheel of Fortune*, a movie, or, on Fridays,
Star Trek. Tonight, what luck, it's the pilot
episode of *Deep Space Nine*, that one where
Captain Sisko visits with Kai Opaka on Bajor
and learns he's destined to become The Emissary.
Here's the part where Sisko stares into the Orb
of Prophecy and Change, which always catches

the Prophet off-guard, a lump welling in his throat.
And soon the scene he can't make it through
without weeping: the Wormhole Aliens disbelieving
Sisko's temporally linear existence as he stands
before them tortured by memory, caught between worlds.

THE PROPHET ON CAMPUS

On a fluke summer day in late fall,
students fling Frisbees, loll on grass,
their books strewn, basking in last sun.
Walking in his black suit across
the grounds, the Prophet pauses, hearing
through open windows a little *Paradise Lost*,
some astronomy, a debate on the world
economy. Smiling, a stack of books in hand,
he makes his way to the top step outside
the ivy-covered library. Looking over
the passing crowd he wastes no time,
imploring: *My people, let us consider*
now these shadows thrown across the day...
As he speaks, he glides between topics—
a virtuoso professor delivering ideas
with great care. Every so often he's sure
his eyes have met those of a student, bound
to inquire where he's going with "*each toward*
our hidden citadel" or "*shredded, though with*
universal thread our new flag woven..."
but instead they march by with their headphones
on, or sit on the lawn lost in an ancient play,
their cells buzzing with neglected texts
and calls. Later that night, most classes over,
only stragglers rush past still somehow unmoved
by the Prophet's lecture, his voice now haggard.
His earlier oratorical luster worn, he now meanders
in one utterance from peak oil to Punxsutawney Phil,
from genetic mutants to *American Idol*.
Determined, the Prophet continues for hours,

the campus bell tower tolling midnight,
as in a hushed voice he speaks for those
who might assemble to listen and learn, the library's
yellow light throwing his shadow down long stairs
onto the empty benches, the empty lawn.

THE PROPHET AT THE POETRY READING

Across campus in late day autumn light,
the Prophet walks toward the academy's hall
where this evening one of the nation's great
unknown poets will recite his verse. All

these devotees: a line of students files
through pillared stone archways into the dim
nave of the auditorium. As the last seats fill,
the Dean completes his intro, a list of acclaims

and honors setting the tone. A little thrown
by the first poem, something about the way
light lies, the Prophet fades, the unfaltering drone
of the poet's voice and audience moans swaying

him into sweet sleep. Hours later, the pews
empty, drool pools on his black suit. He snoozes.

THE PROPHET IN THE WAR ZONE

After accepting his mission, the Prophet
ducks behind a metal wall as a band
of terrorists charges toward him
well-armed. New to this war, he reaches

for his rocket launcher, firing one
high and wide, unleashing his enemies'
first firestorm of bullets, one killing him
easily. Next round, he grips his guncon

harder, plants his feet firmly, takes aim
with an Uzi, spitting a barrage of gold
orbs toward the terrorists, taking out
ten on top of a building, ten more

down a graffiti-scrawled alley, two or three
behind a burning car, one point blank
after turning toward headquarters for ammo.
The more his enemies scream and grunt,

blood spurting from their necks and mouths,
the higher his score, the deeper the stakes,
the darker the game. The next level displays
the city at night, mosques and temples

glowing under a sky ablaze with rockets.
Sneaking into the city center, the Prophet
holds his trigger, feels grit under his feet,
hears whispering nearby, so turns

in his black suit to look at the other soldiers
in this strip mall arcade: a firing line of high
school kids, mostly, but some even younger,
all stone-faced, shooting plastic guns

into monitors at their own hyper-real battle
scenes, firing, reloading, firing, their eyes
darting from fresh kills to their stats, their
time remaining. Blinking lights, bombs,

digital screams, coins rattling in the change
machine—the arcade chaos takes the Prophet
out of his game, aghast at the stern eyes
of the children fighting beside him. Averting

his gaze from the war proves fatal as he finds
in turning toward his machine that he has died
a few more times in that other world. Peering
back into the glass screen, the Prophet's face

is a fractured mess, the twisted visage a soldier wears
when he's seen too much and cowers somewhere
twitching in a heap, a tangled puppet pulled
offstage. Over the reflection of his face,

bright red and blatant, flash the words
GAME OVER GAME OVER GAME OVER
GAME OVER GAME OVER GAME OVER
GAME OVER GAME OVER GAME OVER.

THE PROPHET AND THE SEABIRD DREAM

Here comes the Prophet beyond the empty
shore town road, walking barefoot toward
the beach in his black wetsuit at sunrise,
dragging his old-school long board, stoked
to scope some gnarly tubes offshore.
South of the pier he spies a spot with killer crests
to shred, decides that's the beach he'll terrorize.
In another world, he's drifted off in his easy chair
toward the end of *The Endless Summer*,
but here he's the one God in search of the perfect
wave to glide. As he approaches the water,
his jaw drops. All along the abandoned shore,
tossed in froth and blood, hundreds of seabirds
float. Bludgeoned, eyeless, most bound with rope
and shot repeatedly, the tortured birds tumble ashore
to a humped mess of matted feathers on mud.
Off the pier, four fishermen free snagged birds
from nets, pointing and yelling in Arabic, trying
to retrieve one bird somehow still living
though its wings are slashed to bits. *What coast is this,*
what ocean, whispers the Prophet, aghast,
to one of the men who walks back up the beach
to puke and spit, the reek too much to bear.
Looking up at him, the fisherman says *Everybody's gone*
surfin'...before turning back toward the sea.
Watching him walk away, the Prophet sees

the Pacific is not the Pacific but the Tigris,
the birds not birds but butchered men.
Everyday there are more, say the fishermen,
reeling in another riddled body, rising from
the turbid current into the light.

3

THE PROPHET IN THE HEARTLAND

Standing in his black suit, the Prophet's the sole
disturbance on the horizon in every direction,
the only upward mark on that flat line drawn

between miles of land and sky. For hours
he stands watch over the fields, waist high
in a sea of seeded gold as long winds heave

the waves of wheat. Like a country doctor
caught without his bag of glistening instruments,
he has no stethoscope to listen to the heart

of this body but his ear, with which he listens
first for the breathing, later for the rhythm
beneath the wind. In the bruised light

of sundown, he lies between the stalks,
presses his ear to the dark ground and listens
for an hour to a broken cadence in the pulse.

Distant at first but growing steadily,
an irregular thrum, the nation's deep drum
plays an audible awful offbeat, the ground note

gone beneath a growing roar. Patient, he listens
with great hope to hear the familiar lub-dub restored,
but knows by this strangely grinding motor

in the blood of the country, the diagnosis grim.
There's nothing worse than feeling a body dying
beneath you than to have to share this news,

but brave, the Prophet rises in the field
facing north, rehearsing the words he'll bring
to his people: *This is the most difficult part of this work,*

but I want to be as direct as possible because you'll need
to decide how you'll proceed. After my examination,
I'm afraid my worst suspicions have been confirmed...

But as he stands, a huge shudder wells in his chest
as he hears the roar torn from the flesh of the Earth
and turning, stares directly into the mouth

of a thresher, it's silver blades thrashing the grasses,
a machine big enough to make minced meat of him.
An invisible blackbird to the driver,

the Prophet dives out of the way, barely landing,
safely cushioned on a pile of crushed wheat.
Watching it pass, its glint of giant scalpels

slicing a wide swath through the crop, he places
his shaking hand beneath his lapel, feels
the unmistakable quaking there.

THE PROPHET AT THE INDUSTRIAL COMPLEX

The Prophet half wonders if the world's
packed up and left. On a bright afternoon, he stands
in his black suit beside the smooth cement
of the drained reservoir behind a factory.

A sunken warship, its eight steel smokestacks
are cannons aimed at the blue sky.
No one's anywhere. In the empty parking lot,
a seagull lands on a sign: *Assembly: Evacuation*

Location. Commanding the bird's attention,
the Prophet lifts his arm and points toward the ocean,
somewhere 600 miles east. Stern-eyed, it looks
away, so he lowers his arm, knowing the way

cannot be shown to those who prefer being
lost. Beside the reservoir shines a small field
of phosphorescent grass, a plot doused electric green
by sprinklers—as if someone's trying to save

one last patch of a living planet. Beyond this, a paved
landscape stretches for miles like an abandoned city
with its framed fortresses of steel beams and wires.
A network of yellow pipes vanishes into the horizon,

huge generators hum behind barbed wire. Miles into
the distance, high-voltage towers loom like giant robots
holding hands. Even the wind's restrained.
Noticing the gull's flown, and to fight the sudden

feeling of being left alone, the Prophet turns toward
the factory and unleashes his fire, shouting:
I won't be made extinct by your machines!
The great trumpet call of his voice pings foolish

and aluminum against the corrugated side
of this fortress. Watching from high ramparts,
the many eyes of laser-guided cameras turn toward him,
recording in miniature each thrust of his defiant fist.

Reaching deeper into his heart's cauldron of molten ore
he finds a voice loud enough to rouse great winds
and so begins again, screaming: *I will not be made...*
muted by the screech of giant fans on the building's side.

Turning in a slow whoosh, soon the propellers'
full bellows begin, swallowing his voice,
inhaling dust from the land, stealing
wind from the whirling currents of sky.

THE PROPHET ON THE MOUNTAIN

Late August and the long dead grasses
lean as the Prophet ascends into
downward gusts, nearing the peak.
Climbing toward towering storm clouds,
he wonders if some god or demon
doesn't want him here, wants to pluck him
like a beetle off this face, to send him tumbling

in his black suit back down to the street,
but he continues, half crawling.
He'd come looking for a mountain
on which to claim a sprawling view,
but out beyond the freeway, this huge hill
will have to do. What once were specks
from down below, like fleas leaping on and off

a sleeping beast, these mad seagulls now dive
at his eye level, more like vultures or devils
descending in rings today's infernal air.
Why they've come to call this home
the Prophet can't tell, unless beyond this hill
there's some heaven of an ocean horizon
they lead him to. Reaching the crest,

the Prophet teeters in a sudden rush
of torrid steam, as if on the smoldering lip
of a volcano soon to blow. Staring into
a cavernous mouth of trash, crumbling cliffs
of layered waste, he watches the gulls,
these wayward angels lift and flutter
like flakes of ash from an incinerator,

feeding on filth as a fleet of dump trucks
drops their jaws to deliver another load,
making these scavengers shriek. One bird
soars near, and the Prophet turns to watch
its low sweep over the face that hides
this view of a world laid waste from the new
suburbs, before coursing south over

that dark river—the freeway that flows
through scattered developments,
green lawns and strip malls, then spills
toward the blink of barely visible fires,
the pyres and smokestacks of industry,
over the chewed up streets to land
somewhere in the city's gutted core.

THE PROPHET AT THE TRAIN STATION

Sleek as an alley cat in his black suit, the Prophet
slinks through a hole in the chain link fence
arriving at the battered station steps. Central depot
of a once-bustling city, now this vacant station's
a grandiose wreck, a ghost-house welcoming no one.
Hello…hello…hello…is there anybody in there,
the Prophet yells, his voice echoing long empty halls
in reply. Gutted by years of vandals and winters,
this ruin's many stories of shattered windows admit
a splintered light. Pigeon shit caked on the lobby's
broken mosaic arches, scrawled graffiti and shed
feathers falling, the station still welcomes the arrivals
of scavengers and rats. Stepping through dumped
and windblown trash, the extinguished fires
of broken souls who nightly call this home,
the Prophet makes his way to the platform,
back out from the shadows into the bright day
of the yard. Tree branches wave from car windows
in a row of rusted engines; scattered flowers and grass
stand tall where steel tracks once lay. Startled birds
burst from vines in barbed wire as the Prophet,
playing conductor, cups his hands to his mouth,
shouting across this hidden wilderness:
All passengers must exit, he hollers, *this is the end
of the line.* And in some distant year they hear him
and disembark, a trainload of wraiths stepping through
clouds of steam: a family of immigrants burdened
with bags and a desperate hope, soldiers returning
to a crowd of cheers and thrown confetti, each traveler
having reached their destination: this new station
a glistening gateway to their destiny, their nation.

THE PROPHET ENTERS THE WILDERNESS

Half blinded by the city's din, the Prophet
follows signs on the highway overpass
toward the forest. Hours and miles of nothing
but his shoes scuffing along the roadside,

he turns to look back at the metropolis,
the clouds above it tainted with eerie light.
Leaving the roadside, he climbs over
a guardrail, loses his footing and tumbles

down an embankment in his black suit, stopped
by a boulder at the foot of a huge pine.
Peering into the near darkness at giant trunks,
he might be in some temple's endless pillared hall.

Standing, he aches and stammers, hungering
for solace, some cave or quiet core, a place
to listen to the wind, the crackle of his inner fire.
Soon he finds a pristine spot, clears some brush,

bivouacs riverside. For three days, nothing
disturbs the Prophet but burbling water and birds,
as he plucks berries and nuts from a bag of trail mix
he bought at the gas station before his rustication.

On the third night, while meditating on the message
he hopes to bring his people, from nowhere
a pinpoint light opens in the distance, splits
into two angelic circles gliding toward him.

Then another pair of lights, and another.
Oh let this vision not deceive me, the Prophet
whispers, standing ready to receive them,
to commune with these celestial dignitaries.

In a great flash, the light's upon him as he falls
to his knees beneath a floodlit cloud of dirt
lifted by this caravan: a pickup and two ATV's
rush past on a road beside the river he hadn't seen.

Speeding past, they're gone as fast as they'd come,
heading for the State Park campground exit
a mile away. Standing again, the Prophet
catches a spark from the corner of his eye,

a near glow beneath a small bush beside his camp.
Walking toward it, the bush ignites—throwing
flames into the brush, a quick snake of fire
toward his feet. Frantic, the Prophet dances

madly, stamping the burning brush, until—
sweat-drenched and smoked, his black pants
singed, he exhales, hoping he's put out
these embers from a tossed cigarette.

THE PROPHET'S THIRD DREAM

From miles around a crowd gathers
at daybreak, standing silent
in an open field, waiting for

the Prophet to arrive. Walking toward
them, his black wingtips gleam
with dew, as he gropes to part

silver curtains of a slowly lifting fog.
Emerging, he stares at his mute audience,
a wide sea of faces row after row

turning their eyes to him, blind
to what he sees so clearly floating
just above their heads: the horizon

a long orange horror of suicides—
ten million snapped-neck birds
hanging from threads. Dangling

from a broken sky of low cumulus
clouds, the birds spin like hooked fish
or ornaments, their bodies translucent

and luminous, frail as paper lanterns
twirling in the breeze. *If there is
any question*...the Prophet begins,

with no voice, to say to his people,
with his voice lost in that other world
back where his tongue now rests

in his mouth, settled in its wet nest
of sleep, in that world where his eyes
begin to open, half blind again, unable

to see what another waking fog obscures:
ten million tangled answers swaying
over him in the half light of his room

as he wakes to the mirror and clock,
his black suit on its hook,
the window's thin braids of rain.

4

THE PROPHET AND THE WAVE OF ADORATION

Searching for a pair of new black wingtips, the Prophet
strolls through the upscale mall, no longer able to bear
his worn soles. The only shopper in a store stocked
with hip overpriced footwear, overhead speakers

thumping him with an incessant dance beat, he knows
after eyeing a few price tags he'll need to return
to his thrift store close to home. A couple feet away,
the lone spike-haired clerk cracks gum, spies him warily.

Looking up, the Prophet begins, shouting above
the music: *What will be the cost of this distance
between us in the end—across this expanse of merchandise…*
to which the clerk replies, seeing his lips moving: *Huh?*

They're $149. Huh? Yeah, we like don't have your size.
So the Prophet leaves, wandering into the marbled
shopping maze, dazed by fountains, and headless
mannequins clad in deluxe finery. As he stands,

marveling at soaring glass ceilings, the doors burst
open and from the other end of the mall a wave
of ecstatic fans heads straight for him. Stunned,
he turns to address the giddy mob, standing proud

in his black suit, saying: *Finally, my people, my dear listeners...*
when they rush around him, racing toward the indoor
courtyard, where this week's super pop star breaks
into song—a free promo show on her tour of malls.

From where the Prophet stands, watching the back
of his would-be crowd dash around the corner to their star
writhing on a temporary stage, her voice cascades
like tinsel layered and shimmering, a trick of the light.

THE PROPHET'S NEW VOICE

For Assistance Press Here, the sign
over the empty counter reads, so after
several minutes of waiting and no sign
of help, the Prophet presses the lit buzzer.
Hearing his distress signal, the superstore
ceiling speakers emit a calm computerized
command: *Customer assistance*
to electronics…Customer assistance…
As he waits, the Prophet surveys
the megaphones, their plastic trumpet horns
pointed at him from the shelf. By their names
alone—Big Mouth, Mega Horn, Storm Vox—
he knows these instruments will help him
reach his people. After several more minutes,
and the late night store aisles nearly devoid
of shoppers, the Prophet can foresee
that no one will come guide him,
so he reads the specs to take a guess,
and picks the Storm Vox 1000: a 25-watt
model with pistol grip, neck strap, adjustable
volume control, siren and 1000-yard range.
Used for crowd control and military action,
a picture on the Storm Vox box shows
its black horn emerging from flaming clouds,
with the slogan: *They Will Hear You*
Loud and Clear. At the register, he wants to say
to the old cashier whose hand quivers
as he punches buttons: *After the machines*

we will endure, but instead he stands
in his black suit, looking down
as the man bags his Storm Vox and batteries.
Is an extended warranty available?
the Prophet asks, then a second time
even louder, but the man neither nods
nor answers. Leaving the store the Prophet gasps
as a security alarm blasts and two guards arrive
immediately. Looking up as they eye his receipt,
he sees four ceiling cameras trained on him,
one from behind a tinted turret. Reaching into
his pocket he touches his well-worn worry stone,
trying to appear outwardly calm. He thinks
of Detective Mulder on *X-Files*, how steady
he always appears in the face of spies.
The guards seem suspicious but let
the Prophet go, so he enters the night
carrying his treasure to the car where
he can't wait to test it, immediately dropping
batteries into the chamber. Pulling the trigger,
the siren explodes in deafening waves
as the Prophet fumbles the horn and covers
his ears—his car a sudden muffled ambulance
in a vacant parking lot, called to a million
emergencies and none all at once, blasting
with an alarm that he alone can hear.

THE PROPHET AT THE TERMINAL OPENING

At morning rush, the terminal heart's
a flood of frantic passersby. Glass doors
spin, pumping commuters past pillars
into the great city, pulling them from
clogged avenues into this sacred chamber

of comings and goings. Through the entrance
travelers ascend escalators arterial, flow
up capillary stairs, disappear down
interior archways, the clamor of their
onward march a solemn hush

in this vaulted nave. Bumped along
by his people, the Prophet stops
in the middle of this human sea to admire
the soaring ceiling. In his black suit
he stands like a boulder, sees birds dip

high above the crowd in this accidental aviary.
Thumps and cussing, a couple spilled lattes,
bodies course around him, the sea
parted. Cursing into their cells, running late,
they don't see who slows the flow,

they go and go and go. Peripheral lines—
ATM, ticket kiosk, newsstand—block
passages, divert the pulse into errant
channels, pools of brief confusion,
but all, like neutrons en route, return

to their well-known orbits, toward
the shriek of departing trains.
My people, the Prophet whispers,
what song will you hear?
Reaching into his bag, he removes

his megaphone, leaves the case open
at his feet. Amid discordant chatter,
the Prophet decides to sing, to lift
his voice toward the birds, knowing
his most rending falsetto will surely

hush the crowd. At first faint, soon
his radiant voice sways, angelic
and hovering over the headlong
masses. High in towered alcoves,
huddled pigeons cluck, tipping

yellow eyes like satellite dishes
down toward the lone chorister,
this countertenor whose straining aria,
nearing its peak, is suddenly swallowed
in a deluge of monotone

pronouncements: a litany of scheduled
arrivals and departures, uttered once
by the voice of a real woman
who now sings digitally
all day long, never missing a note.

THE PROPHET AND THE JAWS OF HEAVEN

Hand over hand toward the skyward light
the Prophet climbs up a billboard ladder
high above the interstate this winter evening,
his hands trembling on the slicked rungs,

his megaphone hung around his neck.
At rush hour, thousands of passing cars look like
a procession of dark coffins from this height,
he thinks, stretching on for miles, barely budging.

Finally reaching his slippery platform, the Prophet
stands in a squall of glitter, snowflakes flitting
across beams of huge bulbs pointed at the billboard
behind him. On this backdrop a colossal mouth

arcs, a close-up of someone laughing,
their brilliant teeth broadcasting the brighter smile
this toothpaste ad offers. Long foot-thick fangs,
icicles hang from a metal frame over the billboard,

glinting daggers aimed at the Prophet below.
As he steps forward in his black suit
on this metal precipice beside the busy freeway,
lifting his megaphone to speak, his thrown shadow

stains the Great Smile. Anyone looking up
at this moment might see the fleck of him,
and think *that's strange: there's a bit of food
stuck to that model's bottom teeth.*

But will they hear, as, now aiming down
at the cars, the Prophet pulls the trigger
on the handle and from his horn blasts
the hollowed volume of his voice.

Oh, my people, please lend me your ears,
from my humble mouthpiece a common hope...
when startled, the Prophet dives, covers his head
and assumes crash position, buried by a sudden roar:

*thoomp thoomp thoomp thoomp...*the local news
channel's low-flying traffic copter swoops overhead,
its booming engine shaking loose huge stalactites
of ice plunging toward him. Lifting over

the intersection of three freeways, the copter leans
west, its helmeted pilot addressing drivers on their radios
below, telling them what they already know:
that they're stuck. That every way home is slow.

THE PROPHET AND THE BROADCAST TOWER

High winds, a storm cell drifting in, and still
the Prophet stands unwavering in his black suit,
marveling at a gigantic steel mast connected
to dozens of cables. *High Voltage: Do Not Enter*
reads the sign on the fence, but the Prophet
doesn't heed the warning, gripping the fence
to climb it, the megaphone around his neck
knocking against the chain metal links.
Sweaty and sore, he drops to the other side—
looking upward as he takes the first rung
of hundreds, the tower's ladder appearing
as if it leads up into the low clouds. Here
in the Great Plains, the land's a wavering sea,
a vista the Prophet enjoys as he nears,
after a half hour of climbing, the middle
of the tower. Dizzy, he pauses to breathe
and survey the distances—both palms ripped
from the rusted rungs. Far beneath his feet
he sees rooftops of the media complex
from where this huge silver beanstalk sprung,
hears wind whistle the cables like the hiss
of a million invisible transmissions, rivers
of frequencies coursing the sky. Time to climb
higher again, he continues past the red beacon
that flashes to warn pilots, reaching the last
rung and a small platform, where some brave
Neil Armstrong bolted a flag, shredded
though it is, to the pole. The Prophet
might as well be at the top of the world

here, with his megaphone raised to his lips
like a weathervane or copper angel trumpeting
from some old spire. *America, America,*
*come in, America...*the Prophet yells, his voice
resounding as if it might just have reached
the satellites to appear in billions of living rooms,
on radios, TVs, cell phones. Yet here on this
high frequency apex of twenty-four hour chatter
he thinks *what more can be said*, and lowers his horn,
looking out over the land he loves, speechless.

THE PROPHET AND THE SONG OF STOLEN HOURS

Deep in the city's screech and hiss
of brakes, the scattered blare,
the Prophet stands in his black suit,
gone mute and stone-dark in the glare

of breaking glass and bells,
and hears in each urgent note
the clear utterance of a last prayer.
Listen: drain gurgle, stutter of engines,

shuffle of soles and heels,
soot-throated cluck of huddled birds,
the crack and cymbal crash
of machines filling every tunnel

and alley—this dark sea rising
toward the shell of every empty ear.
Listen, my people, he whispers, knowing
the unmistakable decrescendo is here.

Can you hear that? He whispers again
to the crowd of thousands rushing past,
as if they're one and with him
in some quiet upstairs room,

their hearts booming as they hear
first the shattered window,
then the rattling of a lock,
then the foot upon the stair.

THE PROPHET AND THE BRIDE OF HOPE

All half-lost in a gauntlet of fog
and steam-ghosts, skyward ropes
of smoke, a wide horde streams

this evening up the winter avenue,
their faces drawn then erased
in the long-robed float and drag

of fading angels rising from manholes
and grates, from the world beneath
the street. And in this freezing air,

breathing mist from passing strangers hangs
then languishes, as the Prophet stands
and deciphers: here a cloud of clear

despair, there an apparent prayer.
Turning toward the warm blurred glow
of the bridal shop window behind him,

he sees beneath his own dark reflection
the veiled face of a mannequin bride,
her gown an avalanche of lace and silk.

For hours the Prophet stands before her
on the salted sidewalk of this frozen altar
in his black suit, a thin pane of glass

between them. Staring at the marbled eyes
of this fixed beauty, he asks: *Do you see,
my Queen, as I do, through this darkness*

these errant atoms, the glitter of a shattered hope?
Awaiting her reply, snowflakes like silver
confetti fall and settle on his hair, a crown

of little diamonds, but still her painted lips
don't open. Looking down beside him then,
the Prophet sees, mouth upward and open,

a vision of himself as a boy, catching
huge wet snowflakes on his tongue like words
of a bright new language he learns

but soon forgets. Closing his mouth,
the boy turns his face to gaze toward this bride,
like a statue of the Virgin, as if to ask

if she knows this language—before
its giddy epistle dissolves—hoping
he'll hear her healing answer: *I do, I do.*

THE PROPHET'S FINAL DREAM

After the film's fade to black, his remote control
dropped from his limp hand into tipped popcorn,
the Prophet half drowses in his recliner, his wrinkled
black suit over him like a death gown. The film's
ascending credits, then the screen static a hissing

blizzard, and his lids fall. He misses the dream's
arrival in his room: the dark birds, scattered on green
carpet at his feet, falling from his cupboards
and closet, their wings broken, who flail against
his glass door wanting out. In his fevered sleep

a flash—and there they stand, his people, huddled
in a moonlit field. No one moves as he approaches.
Now will you hear my voice, the Prophet asks them,
you who stand in frozen poses, flesh gone to paper,
heads hollowed, hands hung and torn? Those with eyes

gaze in desperation skyward, others stare down
at dying birds strewn across the grass, most stand
trapped in a fragile last sleep. Standing before them
in his black suit, a long winter closing in, the Prophet
knows it's too late for any of them to save the downed

birds, their brittle bodies flaked and breaking.
Before turning to the waking world again, he stands
among them, closes his eyes, and hopes for them to listen
and be stirred: *Bless these standing here in death. Half*
had eyes and chose not to see, half had ears and wouldn't hear.

5

THE PROPHET RETURNS TO THE DRY CLEANERS

In a city like this it's easy to see the dead
still here, to feel their stare as he passes,
looking through the fume-stained square
of a bus window on the cross-town route.
As he sits on the blue plastic seat
cradling his black suit, the Prophet watches
in the fading light of a late winter day
an endless parade: the park bench woman
who daily tears her bread for a clucking
congregation, the dark sockets' downward glare
of the man in his empty shop of lamps
and chandeliers, a passing saint who drops
coins in the bucket of a heaped sidewalk sleeper,
a row of silhouettes staring at machines
in the fluorescent purgatory of a laundromat.
At his stop, the Prophet stands and exits, enters
another rushing stream of strangers, turns to watch
the slumped and silent passengers carried off
to their destinations. Two blocks to the dry cleaners,
with its hand-lettered OPEN sign, its windows
fogged with steam. At the counter, he hangs
his black suit on the hook and waits
for the woman who comes out from the back
to take it away. Today the woman is a girl
who hands the Prophet a pink slip and asks
how he'd like it pressed, lifting his suit
like a superhero's cape or broken wing.
Wanting to take her hand and say *every face we wear
is a withering disguise*, instead he smiles,
says *lightly*, and leaves with his ticket in hand.

ACKNOWLEDGMENTS

Thank you to the editors of the following publications, in whose pages some of the poems in this manuscript first appeared.

Atlanta Review: "The Prophet at the Dry Cleaners"

Listen Up: "The Prophet and the Song of Stolen Hours"

Detroit: "The Prophet at the Industrial Complex," "The Prophet in the Blackout," "The Prophet in the Heartland"

Failbetter: "The Prophet in Flight," "The Prophet at the Summer Fair"

Third Wednesday: "The Prophet and the Bride of Hope"

Thank you to Denise Whitebread Fanning, my wife and the sculptor from whom a few images were inspired (stolen?) from her pieces "Hung Up and Hollow" and "What Should We Do?" Denise, you are my light.

Thank you again to Peter Markus—dear reader, dear friend, dear brother. Thanks to Mariela Griffor and all at Marick Press.

Thank you to Believers since the Dawn: MaryClare Peak and Dan Marlow, as well as those who provided good advice on these poems, including Michael Fisher Jennings, Christina Kallery and Caroline Maun. Thank you to Detroit and the many poets singing there, too many to list here but you know who you are, including all at InsideOut Literary Arts Project.

Thank you to my family.

Readers of this collection are strongly encouraged to purchase the album *He Has Left Us Alone But Shafts of Light Still Grace Our Rooms* by The Silver Mt. Zion Memorial Orchestra and Tra-La-La Band and listen to it while reading with the volume control knob set to the maximum level.

Cover photograph by MaryClare Peak.
Design and typesetting by Daniel Marlow.
Author photo by Denise Whitebread Fanning.

The poems and their titles are set in Minion Pro; the front cover and title page are set in Hypatia Sans Pro; the back cover is set in Arno Pro.

Robert Fanning is the author of *Old Bright Wheel* (Ledge Press Poetry Award 2003) and *The Seed Thieves* (Marick Press, 2006). His poems have appeared in numerous journals, including *Poetry, Ploughshares, The Atlanta Review,* and *Shenandoah.* A graduate of the University of Michigan and Sarah Lawrence College, Fanning's writing awards include a Creative Artist Grant from ArtServe Michigan, the Inkwell Poetry Award, and the Foley Poetry Award. He is an Assistant Professor of Creative Writing at Central Michigan University.

For further inquiries: www.robertfanning.com

LaVergne, TN USA
22 March 2010
176714LV00006B/1/P